MW01138026

A Kid's Guide to
BACKYARD TREES

Felicia Brower

illustrated by
Nicole LaRue

Gibbs Smith

CONTENTS

Welcome to the wonderful world of tree identification! With this table of contents, you can use the shape and type of leaves to help narrow down the names of the trees around you. Here's something important to remember: trees are incredibly adaptable! While the Habitat & Range section will help you figure out what kind of tree you're looking at, you might find the same tree in different parts of the country. So even if a tree is mostly found in the East, don't be surprised if you also spot it out West.

SIMPLE LEAVES

COMPOUND LEAVES

INTRODUCTION

No matter where you live, trees are all around you! They line our streets, fill our parks, and stand tall in forests. Not only are trees cool to look at, they're also really important for our planet. They clean our air, offer cool shade, show off bursts of beautiful color, and provide homes for many animals. Squirrels shelter in their branches, birds create cozy nests and eat berries and bugs, and insects set up shop under their bark. Trees are fun for people to play in too. Have you ever climbed a tall tree, rested against a big trunk to sit in the shade, or watched the colors of the leaves change with the seasons?

Inside these pages, you'll learn how to use the shapes of leaves (from broad and flat to spiky needles), the different types of bark (from smooth to peeling strips), and fruits, nuts, and even sap to identify the different types of trees around you. The best part? You can ID trees anywhere! Whether it's your backyard, the local park, or a hike in the woods, trees will always be there. You don't need any fancy tools—just your curiosity, your eyes, and this handy guide!

Trees might look different in each of the seasons, but there are some features like bark, buds, and tree shape that never change, no matter what time of year it is. With practice, you'll be able to impress your friends and family by pointing out and naming trees that they might never have noticed before.

So are you ready to begin your tree ID adventure? Let's go!

DIY PROJECT

Turn a fallen leaf into a work of art with a leaf rubbing! When you make a leaf rubbing, you make a colorful copy of all of the unique features of that leaf. Remember, only pick up leaves that have fallen—leaves on the tree are still living!

What You'll Need

LEAVES: A VARIETY OF SHAPES AND SIZES IS THE BEST!

PAPER: PLAIN WHITE PAPER SHOWS THE COLORS NICELY.

A HARD, FLAT SURFACE: A CLIPBOARD, TABLE, OR A BIG BOOK WORKS WELL.

CRAYONS: IF THE WRAPPERS ARE TAKEN OFF, IT'LL BE EASIER TO MAKE A COPY.

Look for leaves that have fallen on the ground. Find a flat surface, remove the wrappers from your crayons, and place a leaf under a piece of paper. Make sure the bumpy side of the leaf is facing up so all of the cool details will show on your colorful copy! Hold your paper still with one hand and rub your crayon back and forth over the stacked paper and leaf. As you color, you'll see an outline of your leaf with all of its interesting bumps and lines! If you want a darker copy, press a bit harder with your crayon.

Make It More Fun

→ **Leaf Mix-Up:** Use lots of different leaves on the same piece of paper to make a one-of-a-kind art piece!

→ **Rainbow Power:** Use different crayon colors on the same leaf rubbing.

→ **Leaf Journal:** Keep all of your leaf rubbings together and turn them into a colorful nature journal!

IDENTIFICATION

To find out which type of tree you're looking at, you'll need to look at the tree's **characteristics**. Some important things to know are whether your tree is deciduous or an evergreen and if it is single- or multistemmed.

Deciduous trees lose their leaves every year (usually in the fall or winter) and grow new ones again in spring. **Evergreens** keep their leaves all year long. **Conifers** are common evergreen trees and have needles.

It's also important to know that some trees do not have flowers. **Gymnosperms** are plants that have their seeds out in the open and don't need flowers. These include plants like conifers and the very unique gingko tree.

Single-stemmed trees are trees with one big trunk. Multistemmed trees have several trunks that come from the ground. Smaller trees are often multistemmed if the extra trunks aren't **pruned** by anyone to make the tree a single-stemmed tree.

All trees have common names, which are the names people use in conversation, and botanical names, which are unique scientific names that come from Latin. All plants only have one botanical name, but they can have several common names. The botanical name is always in italics when you're reading it.

The table of contents of this book uses the following questions to help ID different types of trees. Here's what you'll need to know to ID your tree:

CHECK THE LEAVES

- Is there one leaf all by itself on a twig? That's a simple leaf.

- Are there a bunch of smaller leaves on one stem? That's a compound leaf.

- Do the leaves spread out from a stem like fingers from your hand? That's a palmate leaf.

- Is there one long stem down the center with leaves growing out from both sides like a feather? That's a pinnate leaf.

LOOK A LITTLE CLOSER!

- Are the leaves wide and flat? Those are broad leaves.

- Are the leaves very skinny and green? Those are needles.

- Are the leaves tiny and overlapping? Those are scales.

LEAF EDGES

- Do they have pointy teeth? Those are serrated or toothed leaves.

- Can you see big bumps or dips? Those are lobed leaves.

- Are they smooth all around? That's a smooth leaf.

WHAT'S THE LEAF LAYOUT?

- Are the leaves directly across from each other on the twig? That's opposite.

- Are the leaves taking turns on different sides of the twig? That's alternate.

- Are three or more leaves circling a single spot on the twig? That's whorled.

BARK CHECK

- Does the bark feel like a piece of paper? It's smooth bark.

- Are there deep cracks? It's furrowed bark.

- Does it have long, peeling strips? That's shredded bark.

- Does the bark have big squares? Those are plates.

Now that you know the different characteristics a tree can have, use the table of contents to help you discover which type of tree you're looking at.

40 feet tall with a trunk diameter of 8 inches.

EASTERN REDBUD

Cercis canadensis

Eastern redbud trees explode with color in the spring! Tiny, vibrant, pea-like, pink flowers burst out all over the branches. These flowers aren't just pretty, they're a magnet for butterflies and hummingbirds, their long tongues perfect for sipping the nectar deep in the beautiful blooms. The leaves look like giant green hearts in the summer and turn golden yellow in the fall. Even in winter, there's something to see: look for the dried pea pod–shaped fruits hanging from the branches.

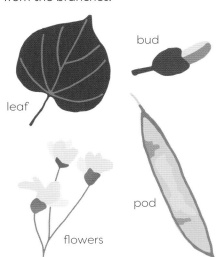

leaf

bud

pod

flowers

■ NATIVE

HABITAT & RANGE

Found all over the country but more can be found on the eastern side of the United States. They prefer rich, moist soils.

BARK & LEAVES

Smooth, dark-gray or brown bark when young that becomes furrowed and scaly as the tree gets older. The simple, 2½- to 4½-inch, heart-shaped leaves have smooth edges.

FLOWERS & FRUITS

Flowers in spring. Small, pea-like, pink flowers are present along the branches and even sometimes the trunk of the tree. Dried, brown fruit pods that look like pea pods hang on the tree throughout winter.

FUN FACT

Their flowers are not just pretty, they're edible too!

SIZE

30 feet tall with a trunk diameter of 8 inches.

FLOWERING DOGWOOD

Cornus florida

Flowering dogwoods are easy to spot in the springtime—just look for long, swooping branches packed with delicate, white flowers. But the show doesn't end there! When summer arrives, the dogwood sports clusters of spiky, bright red fruit—a feast for birds and other woodland creatures. When fall rolls around, the leaves turn a fiery red. Did you know the flowering dogwood is a secret butterfly and moth hideout? Giant silk moths and dazzling Azure butterflies use its leaves as a safe place to lay their eggs, starting an incredible transformation right on its branches.

■ **NATIVE**

HABITAT & RANGE

Flowering dogwoods are found east of central Texas. They like moist or dry soils.

BARK & LEAVES

Dark reddish-brown bark that grows rough plates as the tree gets older. Twigs are often red. The dogwood's 2- to 5-inch simple leaves are smooth but wavy and fuzzy on the underside.

FLOWERS

Flowers in early spring before the leaves grow back. Small, 4-petaled, yellow-green flowers are inside of 1½- to 2-inch, white, petallike bracts.

FUN FACT

Their bracts are incredibly sensitive! Even touching them can cause them to turn brown.

shape

leaf

flower with bracts

SIZE

50 to 70 feet tall with a trunk
diameter of 2 feet.

GINGKO

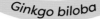
Ginkgo biloba

A living fossil with a stinky secret! Its leaves, like delicate fans, turn a dazzling gold in the fall. But beware the female ginkgo trees—their squishy fruits have a terrible smell! This amazingly tough tree species outlived the dinosaurs and hardly any bugs or animals bother it today. Gingko trees are unique because they're considered **gymnosperms**. Even though the smelly fruits can be a bit of a downside, the gingko nuts inside of them are edible and a very popular treat in Japan!

shape

nut

NATURALIZED

HABITAT & RANGE

Gingko trees do not usually grow wild anywhere in the United States, but they are often found in lawns and along streets. They need humidity and moist soil.

BARK & LEAVES

Young trees have gray bark that becomes rougher and more furrowed as the tree gets older. The simple, smooth, 1- to 2-inch, fan-shaped leaves are in clusters of 3 to 5 and turn a vibrant yellow in the fall.

FLOWERS & FRUITS

There are male and female trees, and the female trees have a 1-inch stinky oblong fruit that turns from green to yellow-orange as it ripens. Gingko nuts found inside the fruit are edible.

FUN FACT

Gingkos are super old! They are the oldest living tree species in the world!

50 to 80 feet tall with a trunk diameter of 2½ feet.

NORTHERN CATALPA

Catalpa speciosa

The big, white blooms of the northern catalpa tree look almost like a watercolor painting. They're splashed with yellow and purple spots and lines to help **pollinators** find their nectar hidden deep inside the flowers. Another easy ID clue for northern catalpa trees is their long, green pods that turn dark brown—they look like giant beans hanging from the branches. Big green catalpa hornworms munch on leaves, only to become targets for parasitic wasps that lay their eggs on the backs of the hornworms, turning them into living nurseries!

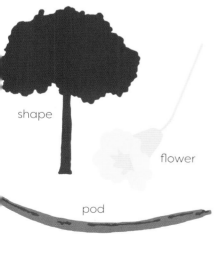

shape

flower

pod

 NATIVE

HABITAT & RANGE

Often found in the eastern two-thirds of the United States. They prefer moist soil.

BARK & LEAVES

Brownish-gray bark when young that becomes deeply furrowed with scaly plates as the tree gets older. Its heart-shaped leaves are smooth and 5 to 12 inches long and 4 to 6 inches wide.

FLOWERS, FRUITS & SEEDS

Flowers in late spring. Large 2-inch white flowers with wavy petals and yellow and purple markings turn into long, green fruit pods that turn dark brown as they mature. The pods split open and have many light-brown seeds.

FUN FACT

Catalpa trees are the only host species of the catalpa sphinx moth!

YELLOW POPLAR

Liriodendron tulipifera

Though not a true poplar, yellow poplars are easy to ID by their leaf shape. These 4-lobed leaves look a little bit like a cat with whiskers. The other easy feature to spot is their eye-catching, tulip-shaped, yellow-green flowers with a bright orange ring around the middle. If there aren't any flowers, look for the duck bill–shaped buds. Because of the flower shape, they're also known as tulip trees!

■ NATIVE

HABITAT & RANGE

Yellow poplars are found in the eastern United States. They like rich soil.

BARK & LEAVES

Young bark is smooth and gray-brown with diamond-shaped markings that darken and get thicker with age. The simple 4- to 6-inch leaves are smooth with a broad V-shaped dip at the center that separates the 4 lobes of the leaves.

FLOWERS & FRUITS

Flowers in spring. The 3- to 4-inch flowers are a yellow-green color with an orange band around the base. The 2- to 3-inch cone-shaped fruit is woody and pointy and has winged, light-brown seeds.

FUN FACT

You have to wait to see the beautiful blooms of the tulip poplar—it takes about 15 to 20 years for the first flowering.

leaf

flower

fruit

19

SIZE

50 to 80 feet tall with a trunk diameter of 2 to 3 feet.

AMERICAN BEECH

Fagus grandifolia

If you spot a tree with smooth, silvery bark; long, pointy buds; and a small, prickly seedpod, it's probably a beech tree. Stand quietly near the tree—can you hear tiny birds chirping their "chick-a-dee-dee-dee" song? Those are black-capped chickadees, and they love making nests in holes inside beech trees. Hungry animals such as deer, squirrels, and chipmunks sometimes stop by for a tasty snack. They love to munch on the little beechnuts found inside the seedpods!

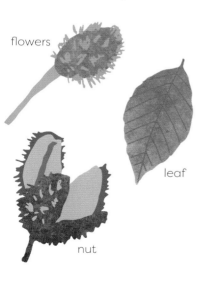

flowers

leaf

nut

NATIVE

HABITAT & RANGE

Found east of Texas and Wisconsin in areas with rich, well-draining soil.

BARK & LEAVES

The American beech tree is one of the few trees that keeps its smooth, light-gray bark even as the tree gets older. Its simple, broad, serrated, 4- to 5-inch leaves have pointed tips. The leaves turn gold in the fall and often stay on the tree during the winter.

FLOWERS & FRUITS

Small, yellow-green flowers appear in early spring but are not showy. The ¾-inch light-brown fruit husks have hooked prickles with 1 to 3 small beechnuts inside that ripen in fall.

FUN FACT

Can you imagine sleeping on a pile of leaves inside your home? Early American colonists used to stuff their mattresses with beech leaves!

SIZE

Usually multistemmed and aroun[d] 20 feet tall with a trunk diamete[r] of 6 inches. Full-sized trees can reach up to 100 feet tall.

AMERICAN CHESTNUT

Castanea dentata

NATIVE

HABITAT & RANGE

They are mainly found where people have planted them. They prefer well-drained, acidic soil.

BARK & LEAVES

Young trees have brown, furrowed bark with horizonal lenticels. The bark turns gray and forms deeper ridges as the tree ages. The simple, serrated, canoe-shaped leaves have many pointy teeth and are 5 to 9 inches long.

FLOWERS & FRUITS

Flowers in early spring. The spiny fruits are found at the end of the twigs. Young fruits are spiny, green, and around 2 inches large. As they ripen, they turn brown and split open, and 2 or 3 chestnuts are inside.

FUN FACT

A single, full-sized American chestnut tree could produce enough nuts to feed a family for a whole winter!

Remember the holiday song that begins with "Chestnuts roasting on an open fire"? Those chestnuts came from this tree! Once a very common tree that could grow to heights of 100 feet or more, full-sized chestnut trees are now harder to find because of a disease called fungal blight that killed many of them. Not to worry—scientists are working hard to bring them back. You can still find smaller, multistemmed trees in parts of the U.S. Chestnuts are an important fat source for bears, deer, and turkeys in the fall.

leaf

young fruit

nut

80 to 100 feet tall with a trun diameter of 4 feet.

AMERICAN ELM

Ulmus americana

Shaped like big, leafy umbrellas, the American elm is the perfect shade tree to relax under. They're also bustling habitats for wildlife! Squirrels, birds, and insects rely on the tree for nesting spots and food. The American elm's flat, coin-sized seeds look a little wacky—they have a small notch at the bottom and hang in clusters along the branches before fluttering down to the ground in the fall and winter.

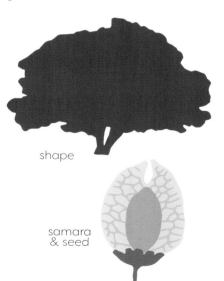

shape

samara & seed

■ NATIVE

HABITAT & RANGE

Often found in eastern North America as far as Texas and the Dakotas. American elms prefer rich, moist soil.

BARK & LEAVES

Light-gray bark with deeply furrowed, scaly ridges. The 3- to 6-inch leaves have an uneven base—one side is smaller than the other! The leaves are double-toothed, which means their teeth have even smaller teeth, and they turn bright yellow in the fall.

FLOWERS & SEEDS

Flowers in early spring. Uniquely shaped green seeds with a red spot at the base. There is a flat-winged cover over the seed, also known as a samara.

FUN FACT

American elm wood is super strong and hard to split, making it awesome for things like hockey sticks and wagon wheels.

SIZE

60 to 100 feet tall with a trunk diameter of 2 to 3 feet.

AMERICAN LINDEN

Tilia americana

Also known as American basswood, American linden trees have big, simple, heart-shaped leaves with one side usually bigger than the other. In the spring, they bloom with bunches of little yellow flowers that look like they're hanging from a leaf. Bees love these flowers, and in spring and summer, it can seem like the tree itself is buzzing! By fall, these flowers turn into small, round nuts. Linden trees are like a bird cafe—nuthatches, finches, woodpeckers, and thrushes love to hang out there. But watch out! Japanese beetles also think these trees are pretty tasty, so you might find them munching on the leaves too.

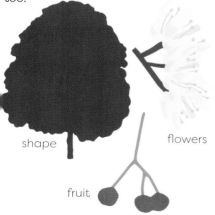

shape

flowers

fruit

NATIVE

HABITAT & RANGE

In the wild, American linden trees can be found east of Nebraska in areas with moist soils. They're often planted as shade or street trees in neighborhoods all over the country.

BARK & LEAVES

Smooth, dark-gray bark when young. Older trees have furrowed and scaly ridges in the bark. The leaves are 3- to 6-inch simple, serrated, heart-shaped leaves with a pointed tip.

FLOWERS & FRUITS

In early summer, yellow-white flowers, with rounded petals that bloom in clusters, emerge. The flowers then develop into small, round fruits that turn brown and fall from the tree in the fall and winter.

FUN FACT

The soft wood of the American linden was once used to make musical instruments like flutes and recorders.

27

SIZE

30 feet tall with a trunk diameter of 1 foot.

AMERICAN PLUM

Prunus americana

In spring, American plum trees burst with clusters of sweet-smelling flowers, but sniff carefully—sometimes those clusters hide sharp thorns! The trees grow in a thick, tangled way, creating a safe haven for birds, squirrels, and even butterflies like the Eastern Tiger Swallowtail. Later in the summer and early fall, the tree grows edible plums that can be purple, red, or even yellow. But don't get too excited about eating them fresh—they're super sour! Instead, these plums are perfect for making yummy jams, jellies, and preserves.

NATIVE

HABITAT & RANGE

Commonly found in the central and eastern United States, but they can also survive as far west as Montana and New Mexico. Prefers moist soil.

BARK & LEAVES

Smooth, gray bark with lenticels along the trunk when young. As the tree gets older, the bark becomes dark brown and scaly. The plum's 2- to 4-inch long, simple, serrated leaves are a dull green, have a point at the end, and two sets of teeth.

FLOWERS & FRUITS

Flowers in early spring before the leaves. The 5-petaled white flowers bloom in clusters of 2 to 5. The plums are usually smaller than 1 inch and the pulp is edible.

FUN FACT

While the pulp of the plum is edible, the seed inside is toxic!

flowers

leaf

fruit

29

SIZE

20 to 80 feet tall (depending on type of birch).

BIRCH

Betula spp.

There are several different types of birch trees (*spp.* in a botanical name means more than one species), but something they all have in common is their unique, horizontally peeling bark that looks like strips of paper peeling off the tree. The bark can be gray, yellow-brown, or even white! When they're young, branches cover the whole trunk, reaching up and down like a ladder. The leaves are triangular with little teeth along the edges, and they shimmer a bright green, sometimes with a silvery underside. Birch trees are a favorite hangout for birds—you might even see sparrows and chickadees building their nests in the branches.

HABITAT & RANGE

Different species can be found all over the United States, but as a whole, they usually prefer cooler areas with well-drained, moist soil.

BARK & LEAVES

Smooth bark that can be brown, gray, or white. The bark peels horizontally as the tree ages. Its leaves are simple, serrated, and have a point at the end.

FLOWERS & SEEDS

Flowers catkins in early spring. Male catkins hang down, while female catkins stand upright and form cone-like clusters. Both are found on the same tree. Birch trees have small, one-seeded samaras.

FUN FACT

Some types of birch twigs taste like wintergreen gum!

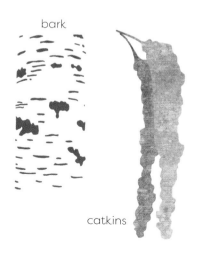

bark

catkins

SIZE

80 feet tall with a trunk diameter of 2 feet.

BLACK CHERRY

Prunus serotina

Black cherry trees put on a show in the spring! Their branches burst with tons of tiny white flowers like a snowy explosion. These **fragrant** flowers aren't just pretty—they turn into juicy little fruits that birds absolutely love! In the wild, you might see turkeys or grouse having a feast. If there aren't any fruits yet, you can still easily ID a black cherry tree. If you crush the leaves or bark, it smells just like a cherry!

flowers

leaves

fruit

■ NATIVE

HABITAT & RANGE

Mostly found east of Texas but sometimes found in Arizona and New Mexico. They can grow in most types of soil.

BARK & LEAVES

Smooth, dark-gray bark with lenticels when young. As the tree ages, the bark turns rough and scaly. The 2- to 5-inch-long elliptical leaves have tiny teeth. The leaves are shiny and dark green on top but light green with a hairy vein underneath!

FLOWERS & FRUITS

Flowers in late spring. Small 5-petaled white flowers hang in drooping clusters and become cherries with dark-red or black skin in the summer. The pulp of the cherry is edible, but the pit is poisonous.

FUN FACT

Birds absolutely love black cherries! Over 70 species of birds eat the fruit.

SIZE

20 feet tall with a trunk diameter of 6 inches.

CHOKECHERRY
Prunus virginiana

When chokecherry trees are in full bloom, they're covered with bunches of tiny white flowers that smell like springtime. But that's not all—those flowers turn into juicy, dark-red berries that are a wildlife feast! Birds such as robins, jays, bluebirds, and catbirds flock to the branches for a tasty snack, and some even build their nests in the tangled branches. Tent caterpillars also love to build their nests in the tree. When winter comes, deer and bears sometimes munch on the twigs and bark when other food is scarce.

leaf

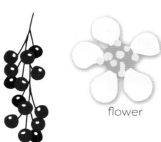

flower

fruit

■ NATIVE

HABITAT & RANGE

These trees can be found all over the United States, but they prefer areas with moist soil.

BARK & LEAVES

Chokecherry trees have smooth, brown or gray bark when young, but it becomes scaly over time. The oval-shaped leaves have very tiny teeth and are dark green on top and light green underneath.

FLOWERS & FRUITS

Flowers in late spring. The ½-inch, 5-petaled white flowers turn into dark-red berries with an edible pulp and a large pit.

FUN FACT

These trees get their name from their strong taste—the berries are super bitter!

100 feet tall with a trunk diameter of 3 to 4 feet.

EASTERN COTTONWOOD

Populus deltoides

Whenever you spot fluffy, white cotton floating through the air in early summer, you know you're near a cottonwood tree. These fluffy seeds float through the air like a gentle snowfall, and the triangular leaves turn into a dazzling display of bright gold in the fall. Eastern cottonwoods are a favorite of majestic bald eagles, who build their enormous nests high up in the branches. It's like a treetop kingdom for these powerful birds!

NATIVE

HABITAT & RANGE

Found east of Idaho in moist, well-drained soil.

BARK & LEAVES

When a cottonwood tree is young, its bark is a shade of yellow-green. As the tree gets older, the bark turns light gray and deeply furrowed. The 3- to 7-inch triangular leaves have rounded teeth, which turn a bright gold color in the fall.

FLOWERS, FRUITS & SEEDS

Flowers in early spring. The 2- to 3½-inch catkins become long strands of fruit pods that are filled with cottony and fluffy seeds.

FUN FACT

Eastern cottonwoods are one of the fastest-growing trees in North America. They can sprout several feet in just one year!

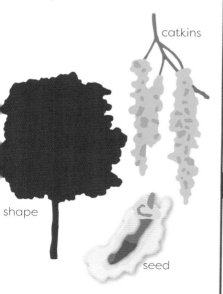

catkins

shape

seed

SIZE

50 to 90 feet tall with a trunk diameter of 1½ to 3 feet.

NORTHERN HACKBERRY

Celtis occidentalis

Have you ever seen a tree with branches growing in a bunch of different directions! That's a hackberry tree! Its branches can grow all twisted and tangled, and sometimes they even curve back toward the trunk. Look out for lots of little bumps on the leaves too. These are called **galls**, and they're made by little insects. They might look yucky, but they don't hurt the tree! Cardinals, mockingbirds, robins, and ducks love to feast on the tree's berries, which look like little raisins when they dry up.

flower

fruit

leaf with galls

■ NATIVE

HABITAT & RANGE

Found in the eastern and mid-western United States north of Georgia and east of Colorado. They prefer moist soil.

BARK & LEAVES

Smooth, gray or light-brown bark that gets corky ridges when it gets older. The simple, serrated, 2- to 5-inch leaves have a lopsided base and a long, pointed tip. They are shiny green on top and pale and hairy underneath.

FLOWERS & FRUITS

Flowers in early spring. Tiny green flowers appear at the base of the leaves. Small orange-red fruits mature and turn purple.

FUN FACT

The texture of hackberry bark sometimes leads to a condition called "witches' broom"—when a cluster of branches grows tightly together, forming a giant broom in the tree!

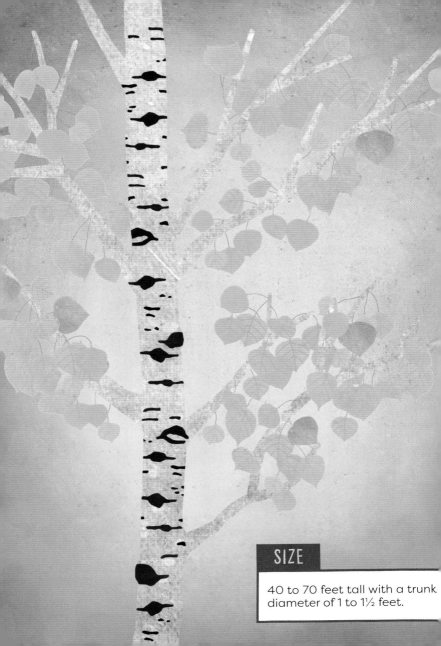

SIZE

40 to 70 feet tall with a trunk diameter of 1 to 1½ feet.

QUAKING ASPEN

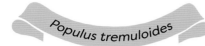
Populus tremuloides

Quaking aspen trees seem to glow—their smooth, ghostly white trunks gleaming in the forest. Look closer and you might spot dark marks that look like eyes staring back at you. In fall, the aspen's rounded leaves turn a dazzling gold, transforming the entire forest into a shimmering spectacle. But here's the coolest part: Aspens aren't just a bunch of individual trees. A **grove** of aspens is actually one giant organism, connected underground by a massive root system! They can even "talk" to each other—sharing water and nutrients and even sending signals about disease, drought, or bug attacks.

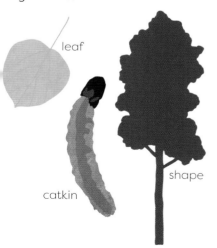

leaf

catkin

shape

NATIVE

HABITAT & RANGE

Grows in the east and west United States, but not in the south past Virginia or the top of Texas. They are often found in big groves out west.

BARK & LEAVES

Smooth, white bark that develops dark spots as the tree ages. Finely toothed 2- to 3-inch leaves are thin and round with a point at the bottom.

FLOWERS

Flowers in early spring before the leaves appear. Hanging male catkins, 1 to 2½ inches long, hang from the tree.

FUN FACT

Quaking aspens get their name from their leaves, which flutter and "quake" in even the slightest breeze.

SIZE

30 to 50 feet tall with a trunk diameter of 3 to 6 feet.

WILLOW

Salix spp.

The willow tree is a water-loving species with a unique, graceful form. Its leaves are slender and pointed, resembling tiny blades that curve subtly along the branches. In springtime, the willow bursts with soft, yellow catkins that release clouds of pollen. More than simply beautiful, willows are vital to their ecosystems. Birds such as robins, blackbirds, and owls find shelter and nesting sites among the willow's dense foliage. Larger animals, such as elk and moose, browse on its leaves, making the willow a valuable food source.

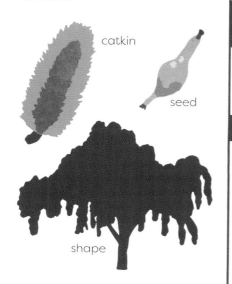

catkin

seed

shape

■ NATIVE

HABITAT & RANGE

Found mostly in the eastern United States but they can live anywhere with moist soil.

BARK & LEAVES

Gray or brown bark becomes deeply ridged as the tree ages. Simple 2- to 4-inch serrated leaves are long, narrow, pointed, and often curved.

FLOWERS, FRUITS & SEEDS

Flowers in spring. Long catkins hang from the tree and become small, round fruit and tiny cottony seeds.

FUN FACT

Willow branches are super bendy and were traditionally used for weaving baskets and making furniture.

43

60 to 100 feet tall with a trunk diameter of 2 to 4 feet.

AMERICAN SYCAMORE

Platanus occidentalis

Imagine a tree with bark that looks like army camouflage. Somehow it makes them easier to spot! The leaves of the American sycamore are big and shaped a little like maple leaves. The spiky fruit balls hanging from their branches are full of seeds that birds such as goldfinches, chickadees, and juncos love to munch on. Even bigger animals sometimes call sycamores home. Look closely and you might be able to spot owls, woodpeckers, and even little birds called chimney swifts building nests inside the trunks of these amazing trees.

leaf

flower

fruit

■ NATIVE

HABITAT & RANGE

Mostly found east of Texas and Wisconsin, but they can grow anywhere in the United States where there is wet soil.

BARK & LEAVES

The bark of the American sycamore is smooth when the tree is young, but as it gets older, its iconic patchwork bark appears with green, brown, and creamy white colors. The simple, palmate leaves are 4 to 8 inches long and wide with 3- to 5-pointed lobes.

FLOWERS & FRUITS

Flowers in spring, but the flowers are very tiny and hard to see. The fruit are spiky 1-inch balls that turn brown as they get older.

FUN FACT

The inside of the tree is often completely hollow!

45

SIZE

Black oaks tend to be smaller in the northern United States! In the south, they grown 50 to 80 feet tall with a trunk diameter of 1 to 2½ feet.

BLACK OAK

Quercus velutina

You can always tell when you're looking at an oak tree if the leaves have big lobes. Black oak leaves have deep, pointy lobes. (Some types of oaks have rounded lobes!) Their acorns aren't that big, and their caps have a fringe that looks a little wild and shaggy. Don't be surprised if you see squirrels, deer, blue jays, and woodpeckers around a black oak—they know those acorns are tasty treats! You might find a soft, orange or brown fuzz covering the underside of oak leaves.

acorn

acorn cap

shape

■ NATIVE

HABITAT & RANGE

Usually found in the eastern United States in drier soils.

BARK & LEAVES

The bark is smooth and gray when the tree is young. As the tree ages, it gets furrowed ridges. Pointy, simple, lobed leaves are 4 to 9 inches long, with 7 to 9 lobes on each leaf.

FRUITS & SEEDS

The acorns are typically smaller than an inch and have caps that have a shaggy fringe. Some oak acorns are edible, but black oak acorns are poisonous to humans!

FUN FACT

The inner bark of the black oak makes a bright yellow dye that has been used for coloring fabric for centuries.

50 to 80 feet tall with a trunk diameter of 2 to 4 feet.

BURR OAK

Quercus macrocarpa

Burr oaks, sometimes spelled Bur oaks, are like treasure chests for wildlife! They have massive acorns—some bigger than your thumb! But here's the coolest part: when colorful birds from the tropics come migrating through, a burr oak tree is one of their favorite bug buffets! They feast on tasty insects like leaf beetles, lace bugs, and even those odd-looking, camouflaged walking sticks that hide in the branches and the bark.

NATIVE

HABITAT & RANGE

Found in the Great Lakes region and the Eastern Great Plains.

BARK & LEAVES

Light-gray bark with thick, deeply furrowed, scaly ridges. The simple leaves are 4 to 10 inches long and 2 to 5 inches wide with 5 to 7 rounded lobes. They're dark green and shiny on top and gray-green with small hairs on the underside.

FLOWERS & SEEDS

Flowers in mid-spring. Male catkins have pollen that is spread to small female flowers on the tree. The acorns are large—up to 2 inches—and have a shaggy-fringed cap that covers most of the acorn.

FUN FACT

Burr oaks have the biggest acorns of any oak tree native to North America. Their acorns can be as big as a golf ball!

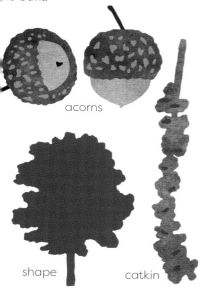

acorns

shape

catkin

RED MAPLE

Acer rubrum

Red maples add a splash of color to any landscape. In spring, they burst with tiny red or yellow flowers, like confetti on its branches. Then come those famous "helicopter" seeds—nature's own little toys, twirling to the ground as the season changes. As summer arrives, its pointed leaves form a lush green canopy. But the red maple saves its greatest trick for autumn, transforming into a whirlwind of fire colors. Reds, oranges, and yellows explode across its leaves, making the tree look like a living bonfire.

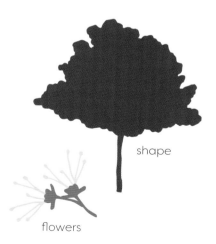

shape

flowers

■ NATIVE

HABITAT & RANGE

Found in eastern and central United States. They like moist soil.

BARK & LEAVES

Thin, smooth, gray bark turns into long, scaly ridges as the tree gets older. The simple 2- to 4-inch-long and wide leaves have 2 to 3 pointed lobes.

FLOWERS

Flowers in late winter or early spring before the leaves come in. Flowers hang in 1-inch-long clusters.

FUN FACT

While sugar maples are the main source of maple syrup, red maples can also be tapped for their sweet sap.

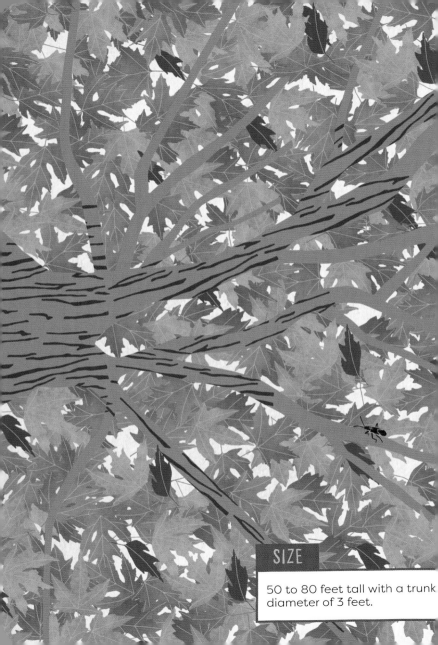

SIZE

50 to 80 feet tall with a trunk diameter of 3 feet.

SILVER MAPLE

Acer saccharinum

■ **NATIVE**

The silver maple leaves stand out from a lot of other maples. The leaves have 5 pointy lobes with sharp edges—they almost look like stars! If you flip them over, you'll see their silver underbelly. In the fall, the leaves transform again, turning from green to a burst of sunshine yellow. Silver maples are like bug magnets, especially for boxelder bugs! These little critters with their black and red or orange markings love to hang out on the tree. One downside of the silver maple is that the bark is weaker, so big branches and twigs often break off of the tree.

HABITAT & RANGE

Naturally east of Oklahoma, but they do not grow in Florida. They like moist soil.

BARK & LEAVES

Gray bark furrows into deep ridges as the tree ages. Silver maple leaves usually have 5 narrow lobes and sharp teeth. The undersides of the leaves are silver or light in color.

FLOWERS

Flowers in late winter. They have short, round, pink or red flower clusters that are usually ½ inch wide. The flowers are often hidden by the red bud scales.

FUN FACT

Silver maples are one of the first trees to flower in the spring!

scales

shape

flowers

53

SIZE

70 to 100 feet tall with a trunk diameter of 2 to 3 feet.

SUGAR MAPLE

Acer saccharum

The leaves of the sugar maple have 5 big lobes, like a hand with outstretched fingers. In the spring, you might spot tiny flowers hanging in clusters, attracting a special visitor—the flying squirrel! These amazing creatures munch on the buds and flowers, and sometimes even nibble on new branches. At the end of summer, the leaves change from green to a whole rainbow of fall colors—bright yellow, fiery orange, and even deep red!

■ NATIVE

HABITAT & RANGE

Sugar maples are found in the northeast United States. They like rich soil.

BARK & LEAVES

This tree has light-gray bark that becomes furrowed with scaly ridges as the tree gets older. Sugar maples have simple, broad, 5-lobed leaves that don't have many teeth.

FLOWERS

Flowers in early spring. Small, bell-shaped calyx appear in clusters.

FUN FACT

Sugar maples are the primary source of maple syrup. It takes about 40 gallons of sap to make a single gallon of syrup!

flowers

shape

SWEETGUM

Liquidambar styraciflua

With leaves that look like giant green stars and seedpods that resemble spiky balls, sweetgum trees look like they came from outer space! In the summer, green star-shaped leaves create a cool, shady hideaway. In fall, its leaves turn into a wild mix of colors! Some glow green, others blaze red and orange, and some even turn a deep, moody purple. And don't forget those spiky balls! They dangle from the branches like prickly ornaments. Hummingbirds sip sweet nectar from its flowers, and giant luna moths, with pale-green wings, start their lives munching on the leaves. A long time ago, chewing gum was made from **resin** found under the bark!

NATIVE

HABITAT & RANGE

Southeast United States. They like moist soil.

BARK & LEAVES

Sweetgum trees feature gray and deeply furrowed bark with narrow, scaly ridges. The 3- to 6-inch, deeply lobed leaves have 5 to 7 lobes and look like stars.

FLOWERS, FRUITS & SEEDS

Flowers in spring. Tiny 1-inch flower clusters become spiky seedpods with 1 to 2 seeds inside.

FUN FACT

If you crush a sweetgum leaf, it releases a sweet, spicy scent.

leaf

seedpods

flowers

57

30 to 60 feet tall with a trunk diameter of 1 to 2 feet.

WHITE OAK

Quercus alba

These amazing trees are usually as wide as they are tall—some have even grown to 120 feet wide (that's as big as 3 school buses!). Just like other oaks, white oaks have deeply lobed leaves—though white oaks are always rounded. The leaves are green all summer but turn brown and stay on the branches of trees through fall and most of winter. White oak acorns are a valuable food source for lots of animals and insects, but they only appear every 4 to 10 years. If you look closely, you might even spot a walking stick hiding in the branches—it's one of their favorite trees!

NATIVE

HABITAT & RANGE

East of Nebraska, but it does not grow in Florida. They can live in a lot of different habitats.

BARK & LEAVES

White oak bark is gray with small plates that become furrowed rectangular blocks as the tree ages. The 5- to 9-inch leaves have 7 to 9 rounded lobes.

FLOWERS & SEEDS

Flowers in mid-spring. Long, green catkins dangle from the branches. The egg-shaped acorns are on the smaller side (under 1 inch) and have a shallow cap and a short stalk.

FUN FACT

White oaks are known for their huge size and can live for centuries—some for more than 450 years!

acorn

shape

catkin

SIZE

70 to 90 feet tall with a trunk diameter of 2 to 4 feet.

BLACK WALNUT

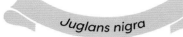

Juglans nigra

It's easy to spot a black walnut tree in the summer—just look for the big, round green fruits scattered on the ground or hanging from the tree. But beware: they'll stain your hands a dark color that is very hard to get off! If you do crack one of the fruits open, you'll find a dark-brown walnut with lots of deep grooves and ridges. Squirrels go *nuts* for these, but the trees have a hidden enemy—hordes of hungry walnut caterpillars!

multiple leaflets from one branch

walnut

shape

catkin

■ NATIVE

HABITAT & RANGE

East of Oklahoma. They grow best in moist, well-drained soil and are usually found near streams, lakes, and other water sources.

BARK & LEAVES

Dark-brown, deeply furrowed bark with lots of scaly ridges. Pinnately compound, finely serrated leaves each have 15 to 23 leaflets. The undersides are usually lighter green.

FLOWERS & FRUITS

Small, green catkins flower in early spring. The 2-inch fruit balls are green before ripening and turning dark brown or black. Walnuts inside the fruit pods are dark brown, roundish, and ribbed with deep grooves.

FUN FACT

Black walnut trees usually grow alone because they release a chemical called juglone into the soil, which can be harmful to some nearby plants.

SIZE

30 to 50 feet tall with a trunk diameter of 12 inches.

BOXELDER

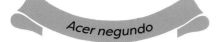

Acer negundo

Boxelder trees are where you'll find those flashy, red-and-black bugs hanging out. Named after the tree, boxelder bugs can swarm the trees in warm weather. But don't worry, they don't hurt the tree! Just like maple trees, boxelder trees have amazing, winged fruits called **samaras**. Samaras hang from the branches and spin like tiny helicopters when they fall. The leaves might remind you of ash trees at first, but boxelder leaves are smoother around the edges.

samaras

leaf

shape

NATIVE

HABITAT & RANGE

Boxelders can be found from New York down to central Florida and as far west as Texas and the plains region. They like moist or wet soils.

BARK & LEAVES

The bark of young trees is light brown with shallow ridges. As the tree gets older, the bark turns gray and the ridges get deeper. Boxelders have pinnately compound leaves with 3 to 5 lightly serrated leaflets per leaf.

SEEDS

They have winged samaras.

FUN FACT

Boxelder trees make a sap that has a lot of sugar. It's sometimes used to make a syrup known as "mountain molasses"!

SIZE

70 to 80 feet tall with a trunk diameter of 2 to 3 feet.

HONEY LOCUST

Gleditsia triacanthos

If you spot a tree that looks like it's wearing armor, that's the honey locust! Be careful when trying to ID this tree: long, sharp spikes cover its trunk and branches. In the fall, its leaves turn gold and flutter down leaving giant, flat, curly seedpods behind. They usually stay all winter—a good thing for the hungry deer, squirrels, and farm animals like sheep, goats, and cows that like these tasty treats when it's cold outside and there isn't much else to eat.

shape

flowers

pod

NATIVE

HABITAT & RANGE

Often found in the central U.S. They like moist soil.

BARK & LEAVES

Gray-brown bark that appears to be peeling off. The long leaves of the honey locust are double pinnately compound with ¾- to 1½-inch-long leaflets that turn golden-yellow in the fall. The leaflets have small, widely spaced teeth that sometimes make them look smooth.

FLOWERS & FRUITS

Flowers in late spring. White or greenish-yellow flowers in 2- to 5-inch clusters have a strong smell. The 8-inch-long dried fruit pods hang from the tree in the fall and winter.

FUN FACT

Want hot chocolate but out of cocoa powder? In a pinch, honey locust pods can be ground up and used instead!

SIZE

70 to 100 feet tall with a trunk diameter of 2½ feet.

SHAGBARK HICKORY

Carya ovata

You can guess from the name, but the shaggy, curly bark on this hickory tree makes it easy to ID! The bark is a perfect hideout for bats, bugs, and tiny critters looking for a safe space to live. The other easy ID clue are the big, green balls that hold delicious, crunchy nuts inside. Animals go crazy for this tasty treat—squirrels, chipmunks, birds, foxes, bears, and even people! If you want to try a hickory nut for yourself, you might have to wait or find an older tree. They don't start making nuts until the tree is at least 40 years old!

■ **NATIVE**

HABITAT & RANGE

Often found on the east coast, north of mid-Georgia, but can be found as far west as Texas. They like moist soil.

BARK & LEAVES

Light-gray, shaggy bark. Pinnately compound leaves of 5 or more serrated leaflets.

FLOWERS, FRUITS & SEEDS

Flowers in mid-spring. Green male catkins hang from the tree, while female flowers appear as spikes. The fruit starts as a thick green ball that turns brown as it ripens and has a light-brown, 4-ribbed, edible hickory nut inside.

FUN FACT

Hickory wood is a favorite for smoking meats! It gives the food a tasty, sweet, and smoky flavor.

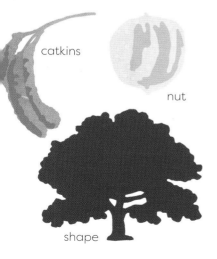

catkins

nut

shape

The smooth sumac can reach up to 20 feet tall with a trunk diameter of 4 inches.

SMOOTH SUMAC

Rhus glabra

Smooth sumac is a wild, shrub-sized tree that puts on a dazzling show. Its leaves look like giant feathers and in the summer, fluffy, sweet-smelling flower clusters attract stunning monarch butterflies with their bright wings. But the real magic happens in fall. The sumac's leaves burst into reds, oranges, and yellows. And in late summer or fall, fuzzy red berry clusters appear, lasting through winter as a tasty snack for hungry birds.

NATIVE

HABITAT & RANGE

Found in all states in areas where there is sandy soil. They're often spotted on roadsides in big groups.

BARK & LEAVES

The brown, smooth bark becomes scaly as the tree grows. The big, 12-inch, pinnately compound leaves have 11 to 31 serrated leaflets as long as 4 inches.

FLOWERS & FRUITS

Flowers in spring. The green, yellow, or white flowers are tiny and hairy. Clusters of small, dark-red berries form in bunches at the end of branches and last through fall.

FUN FACT

This is the only tree native to all 48 contiguous states in the United States!

fruit

flowers

shape

69

80 feet tall with a trunk diameter of 2 feet.

WHITE ASH

Fraxinus americana

The white ash is a favorite snack for hungry tiger swallowtail caterpillars, helping them grow into beautiful, fluttering butterflies. You can ID a white ash by its special U-shaped leaf scars and bark that looks like a pattern of dark triangles. Sadly, a tiny but destructive bug called the emerald ash borer is attacking these incredible trees. But scientists and nature lovers are fighting back, working hard to save the white ash and all the creatures, like the tiger swallowtail caterpillar, that depend on it for survival.

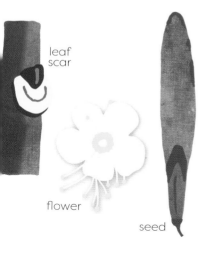

leaf scar

flower

seed

■ NATIVE

HABITAT & RANGE

Found east of Texas, Nebraska, and Minnesota. They like moist, rich, well-drained soil.

BARK & LEAVES

Dark-gray, thick bark with diamond-shaped ridges. The pinnately compound leaves have serrated 2- to 5-inch leaflets in clusters of 7.

FLOWERS & SEEDS

Flowers in early spring before the leaves come in. Small purple clusters of flowers hang from the tree. The seeds are short with a long wing.

FUN FACT

White ash is the wood used to make the famous Louisville Slugger baseball bats!

1 to 4 feet tall but can get up to 25 feet in some areas.

COMMON JUNIPER

Juniperus communis

To spot a juniper tree, look out for blue, dusty, berry-like cones and scaly leaves that actually look like snakeskin! Common junipers look a lot like eastern red cedar, so take extra time when you're making an ID of either tree. You can tell them apart because common junipers stay shorter and their needles stay sharper even as the tree gets old. Juniper trees are an important part of the ecosystem. Their cones are an important food source for animals like rabbits, mice, and various birds. Junipers also provide shelter in their thick, evergreen branches year-round, making them popular nesting sites for species like catbirds, woodpeckers, and bluebirds.

NATIVE

HABITAT & RANGE

Common junipers can be found scattered across the United States, usually north of the Carolinas. They need well-drained soil.

BARK & LEAVES

Reddish-brown bark that becomes gray, thin, and shredded as the tree ages. The needles are sharp and scaly.

FRUITS & SEEDS

Small, dusty, berry-like female cones take 2 to 3 years to mature. Each cone has 1 to 3 pointy, brown seeds inside. Tiny male cones make pollen.

FUN FACT

Some juniper species can be incredibly old. One Utah juniper is estimated to be over 3,000 years old!

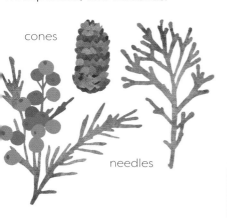

cones

needles

40 to 60 feet tall with a trunk diameter of 1 to 2 feet.

EASTERN RED CEDAR

Juniperus virginiana

With branches covered in tiny, scaly leaves; trunks covered in reddish-brown bark that peels away in long, flaky strips; and berry-looking cones (which aren't really berries at all!), the eastern red cedar might remind you of a juniper tree. They are often mistaken for each other because the eastern red cedar isn't a true cedar at all—it's actually a type of juniper! Their cones are a tasty treat for birds such as the flashy cedar waxwings, cheerful juncos, and those musical mockingbirds. This tree is tough too—it can survive drought, intense heat, and freezing temps!

NATIVE

HABITAT & RANGE

East of Colorado. They can live in almost any type of soil.

BARK & LEAVES

Reddish-brown bark that is shreddy and thin. Small, dark-green, scaly leaves are long and skinny.

FLOWERS, FRUITS & SEEDS

Flowers in early spring. Male cones have pollen. Small, berry-like female cones have 1 to 2 tiny seeds inside.

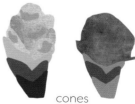

cones

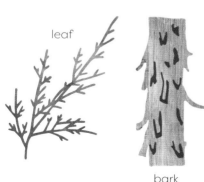

leaf

bark

FUN FACT

People make fragrances from the slightly spicy, woodsy-scented bark!

BLUE SPRUCE

Picea pungens

If the needles are short and sharp, you're looking at a spruce tree! And you can tell you're looking at blue spruce by its color. With a shimmery, blueish glow unlike any other tree, the blue spruce is a standout in any forest. Its branches are armed with 1-inch needles, each one sharp and prickly—a natural defense system and a safe place for birds of all sizes to call home. From tiny songbirds to mighty owls, if you look closely, you can usually find a few different birds nesting in its branches.

NATIVE

HABITAT & RANGE

Commonly found in the Rocky Mountain region. The blue spruce tree prefers wet soil.

BARK & LEAVES

Gray or brown, furrowed, and scaly bark. Evergreen needles are 1 inch long and stiff, found on all sides of the twigs.

FRUITS & SEEDS

The spruce cones are 2 to 4 inches long and stalkless with thin long scales with wavy teeth. Their seeds are on the smaller side but have long wings to help them spread far.

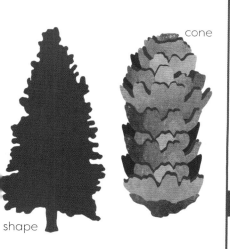

cone

shape

seed

FUN FACT

The tree's bluish tint comes from a waxy coating on the needles.

SIZE

40 to 80 feet tall but can grow
up to 300 feet tall in the wild.

DOUGLAS FIR

Pseudotsuga menziesii

Douglas fir trees have a feature that makes them very easy to ID: look for their pale-brown cones with very long **bracts** peeking out from under the scales. Older trees have really tough, thick, deeply furrowed bark that looks like it could withstand anything. In the wild, these trees can grow to massive heights. Smaller songbirds, such as chickadees and crossbills, rely on the seeds and insects found among the branches, while larger birds, such as the northern spotted owl, use the thick branches for cover and protection.

NATIVE

HABITAT & RANGE

Common in the western United States. Often found in the wild in Idaho, Montana, and Wyoming.

BARK & LEAVES

When the tree is young, the bark is gray and smooth with blisters. Older trees have very deeply furrowed, corky, dark-brown bark.

FRUITS & SEEDS

Male cones are reddish pink and found at the ends of the branches. Female brown cones are about 3 inches long and have very long seed bracts that go far beyond the edge of the cone scales.

FUN FACT

Despite the name, this isn't an actual fir tree! While it's similar to a lot of different conifers, Douglas firs are one-of-a-kind.

shape

cone

seed bract

SIZE

100 feet tall with a trunk diameter of 3 to 4 feet.

EASTERN WHITE PINE

Pinus strobus

The eastern white pine is a super cool tree that both animals and people love. Birds like thrashes, blue jays, and grosbeaks eat the seeds, and even hungry deer and bunnies snack on the needles. Eastern white pines grow really, really tall—sometimes taller than a house! In fact, you might have white pine wood in your home. Because of the size and how light the wood is, construction workers use it quite a bit!

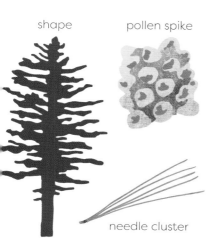

shape

pollen spike

needle cluster

NATIVE

HABITAT & RANGE

North of Georgia and east of Iowa. They like well-drained, sandy soils.

BARK & LEAVES

Gray bark that is smooth when young, but as the tree ages, the bark develops dark, scaly ridges. The straight, blue-green evergreen needles are 4 to 5 inches in length and come in bundles of 5, making it one of the only pine trees with 5-needle clusters.

FLOWERS & SEEDS

Male flowers are pollen spikes. Female yellow-brown cones hold seeds and are 4 to 8 inches long, narrow, and cylindrical.

FUN FACT

Because they're so straight and strong, eastern white pine trees were a popular choice when building ships and bridges.

SIZE

80 to 100 feet tall with a trur
diameter of 2 to 3 feet.

LOBLOLLY PINE

Pinus taeda

With its long, slender needles clustered in groups of 2 or 3, the loblolly pine has a lush, feathery appearance. But be careful: prickly cones hide among the needles. It's the second most common tree species in the United States and really important for the lumber industry in the South. For birds, the loblolly is like an all-you-can-eat buffet. Over 20 different species flock to its branches for a feast of seeds. One bird, the red crossbill, is particularly addicted to the loblolly—these seeds make up half its diet! With its specially shaped beak, the crossbill is a master at prying open those prickly cones.

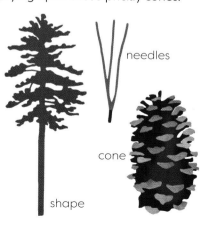

needles

cone

shape

■ **NATIVE**

HABITAT & RANGE

Found in the southeast United States in swampy soil. It can be well- or poorly drained soil, but it always needs to be moist.

BARK & LEAVES

Blackish-gray, thick, scaly bark with deep ridges that show peeks of light-brown bark underneath. Loblolly pines have long 9-inch evergreen needles that come in bundles of 2 or 3 and appear twisted.

FRUITS & SEEDS

The 3- to 5-inch-long, dull-brown cones sometimes have broad prickles at the ends of the scales. The seeds are a little heavier than most pines and have wings to help the seeds spread.

FUN FACT

Loblolly pines are the most common type of pine tree in the United States.

SIZE

20 to 80 feet tall with a trunk diameter of 1 to 3 feet.

LODGEPOLE PINE

Pinus contorta

The tall, slender trunks and branches of the lodgepole pine reach high above the forest floor. But their most fascinating secret lies hidden within their cones. These tough little cones have prickly scales that open after a wildfire sweeps through. This special tree actually needs fire to survive! The flames melt wax sealing the cones, releasing a shower of seeds to start a whole new generation. The burned bark left behind is also a perfect spot for beetles and other insects to hide out in, which attracts hungry woodpeckers in search of a snack.

NATIVE

HABITAT & RANGE

Found mainly in the western United States. Different types of lodgepole pines are found in different areas.

BARK & LEAVES

Light-brown bark that becomes thin and scaly as the tree ages. The 1- to 3-inch needles of all lodgepole pines come in bundles of 2.

FRUITS & SEEDS

The 2-inch egg-shaped cones have a small prickle on the end of each cone scale. Their tiny seeds are released from the cones typically after fires.

FUN FACT

Lodgepole pines have a special relationship with a fungus called blue stain fungus. This fungus gives the wood a bluish-gray tint but doesn't harm the tree.

cone

shape

85

60 to 130 feet tall with a trun
diameter of 2½ to 4 feet.

PONDEROSA PINE

Pinus ponderosa

With its thick, strong branches; extra-long needles; and super-tall, straight trunks, the ponderosa is another tree that is easy to ID when you know what to look for. Scratch a tiny bit of the bark—it has a sweet vanilla or butterscotch scent! The sturdy, well-hidden branches of the ponderosa pine trees shelter creatures of the night, like swooping bats who hang upside down to sleep. Hungry black bears with powerful claws know a secret: they can peel back the bark, revealing a hidden layer of sweet sapwood that tastes like nature's candy.

cone

shape

■ NATIVE

HABITAT & RANGE

Found in the western United States, typically west of Nebraska. They like well-drained soil.

BARK & LEAVES

The bark is usually a cinnamon color and turns into a light-brown, gray, and dark-brown collage as the tree gets older. The flexible 4- to 7-inch needles are evergreen and found in groups of 2 or 3.

FRUITS & SEEDS

The male cones are usually longer and narrower than the female cones, but both can be found on the same tree.

FUN FACT

These are the largest of the western pine species in the United States!

WHITE FIR

Abies concolor

If the needles are flat and flexible, you have a fir tree! The white fir's flat needles are curved and point toward the sky, but the biggest ID trait of a white fir is their stalkless, upright cones that stick straight up from the branches. These cones are treasure chests for birds such as crossbills and chickadees, whose specially shaped beaks are perfect for prying out the nutritious seeds. Even prickly porcupines love gnawing on the bark of the white fir, but their feeding can sometimes damage the tree.

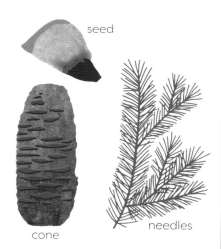

seed

cone

needles

NATIVE

HABITAT & RANGE

Found mostly in the Southwest (south of Idaho) and the Rocky Mountain region. They like moist soils in warm climates.

BARK & LEAVES

Younger trees boast smooth, grayish-white bark. Older trees are dark and thick at the bottom with deep ridges. The flat and flexible evergreen needles curve upward and are 1½ to 2½ inches long.

FRUITS & SEEDS

The 3- to 5-inch cones are green, purple, or yellow and stand straight up from the branches. They have paired seeds with long wings.

FUN FACT

If you crush a white fir needle, it releases a fresh, citrusy scent.

MY TREE LOG

Here you can keep track of all the trees you have spotted. In the Notes column, add details about the tree's appearance and if you see any wildlife around it.

NAME OF TREE	DATE	LOCATION	NOTES

NAME OF TREE	DATE	LOCATION	NOTES

CONSERVATION

Trees are like superheroes for our planet—they help us in so many ways! On hot summer days, trees are our shady saviors, serving as giant umbrellas to keep us cool. They function as huge hotels for all sorts of amazing animals, from squirrels and birds to raccoons and bugs! They operate like giant air filters, using their leaves to clean the air we breathe and make oxygen.

And that's not all—trees also help fight climate change by taking in carbon dioxide, which is like a blanket that traps heat on our planet. Trees keep carbon dioxide stored inside of themselves, instead of out in the atmosphere.

We need trees to have a healthy planet! Here are a few ways you can protect the trees at home:

→ **Plant trees:** Help plant a tree in your yard or ask if your school could plant one! Even a tiny tree can make a difference.

→ **Recycle:** Paper is made from trees. Used, recycled paper can be made into new paper instead of having to cut down more trees for new sheets.

→ **Don't waste paper:** Use both sides of the paper when drawing or writing.

→ **Walk or bike:** Cars cause pollution that can hurt trees. Walking or biking helps keep the air cleaner and gives the trees a break.

→ **Spread the word:** Tell your friends and family why trees are amazing! The more people who know, the more people will help protect them.

GLOSSARY

bracts   Leaves that sometimes look like colorful petals on a flower, but they're not the real petals.

calyx   The green, leafy part at the bottom of a flower that protects it when it's a bud.

catkins   Long, fuzzy flower clusters that hang from some trees.

characteristic   A feature or quality of something that can identify it or set it apart.

conifers   Common evergreen trees that have needles.

deciduous   Trees that lose their leaves every year and grow new ones again in the following cycle.

evergreens   Trees that keep their leaves or needles all year long.

fragrant   Something with a nice smell.

galls   Bumps or growths on trees or leaves made by insects.

grove   A group of trees growing close together.

gymnosperms   A cool type of plant that makes seeds without flowers (think pine trees with cones).

lenticels   Tiny bumps on a tree's bark that help it breathe.

native   A plant or animal that naturally lives in a certain place.

pollinators   Animals, such as bees and butterflies, that carry pollen from flower to flower helping plants make seeds and fruits.

prune   When someone carefully cuts off some branches to help a tree grow stronger and healthier.

pulp   The soft, squishy part inside fruits.

resin   Sticky sap from a tree.

rich soil   Healthy soil full of nutrients.

samaras   Winged fruits that hang from the branches and spin like tiny helicopters when they fall.

showy   Something that's really bright and easy to see.

well-draining soil   Soil that lets extra water flow through easily so the plant's roots don't get too soggy.

First Edition
29 28 27 26 25   5 4 3 2 1

Text © 2025 by Felicia Brower
Illustrations © 2025 by Nicole LaRue

Published by
Gibbs Smith
570 N. Sportsplex Dr.
Kaysville, Utah 84037

1.800.835.4993 orders
www.gibbs-smith.com

Designed by Renee Bond
Manufactured in Guangdong, China in November 2024
by RR Donnelley Asia Printing Solutions
This product is made of FSC®-certified and other
controlled material.

Library of Congress Cataloging-in-Publication Data: 2024939893
ISBN: 978-1-4236-6801-5